The Adventures of

Sherrie and Chubbie 3

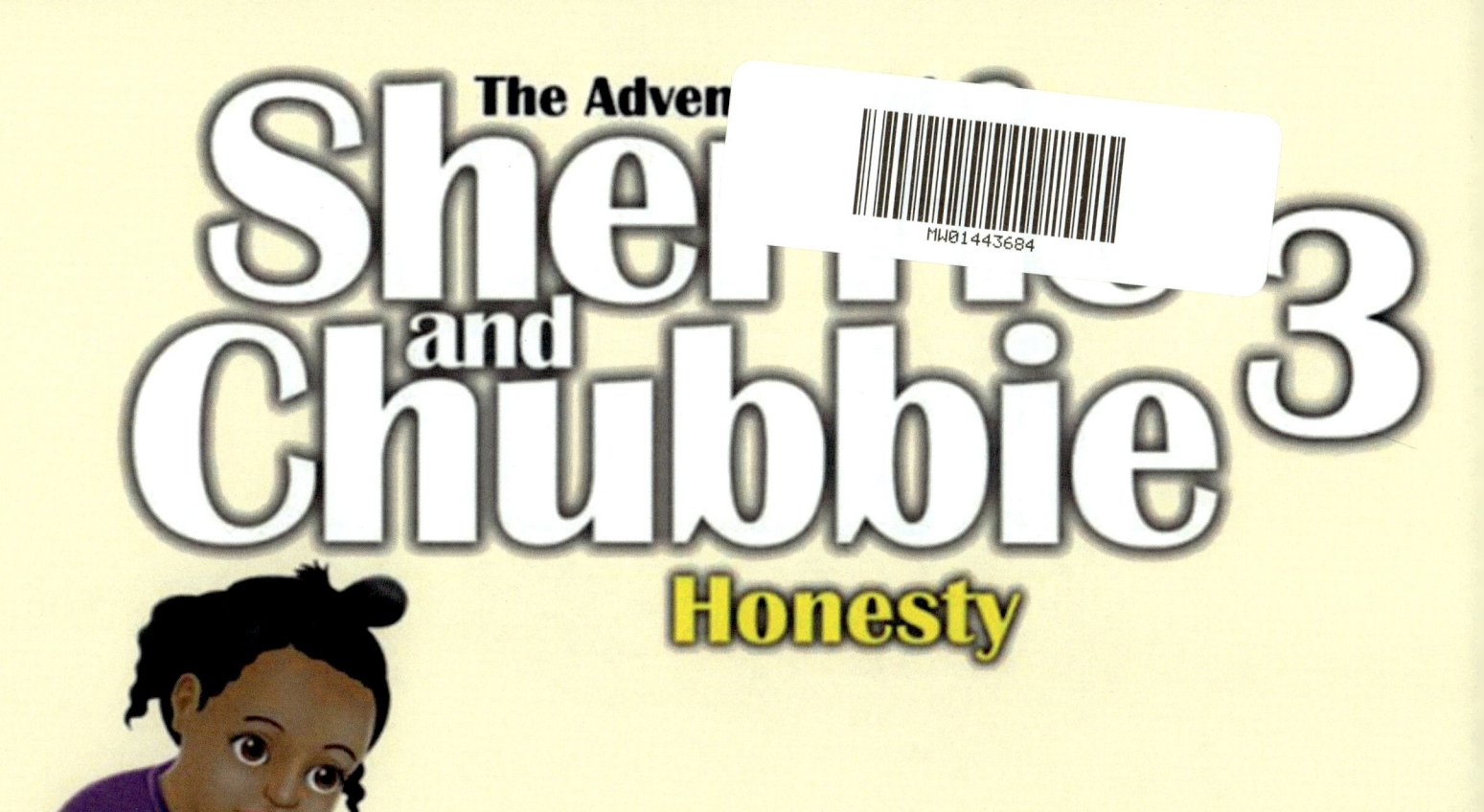

Honesty

by
Sherrie Poitier-Liscombe, Ph.D.

Illustrations by Mike Motz

The Adventures of Sherrie & Chubbie 3: Honesty

Copyright © 2019 by: Dr. Sherrie Poitier-Liscombe

All rights reserved. No part of this book may be reproduced or transmitted in any form or by any means, electronic or mechanical, including photocopying, recording, or by any information storage and retrieval system, without permission in writing from the publisher.

ISBN: 9781797593043

Printed in the United States of America.

The Adventures of Sherrie and Chubbie was inspired by a story written in the early 1980's by my mom, Carolyn Brown Poitier. After publishing the first adventure, I was inspired by readers to create additional adventures. In the past year, I have written a series that takes stories from my life that highlight my counseling personality and provides a platform for my experiences with youth to come to life. Even as a child I was a peer counselor and Sherrie & Chubbie's future adventures teach children good character through rich stories. Each book will model positive relationships, how to overcome obstacles, and will demonstrate how even at a young age, children can use their God given gifts to inspire, encourage, and educate about faith, love and perseverance. This series is dedicated to the youth that keep me focused and aspiring to find ways to change lives every day!

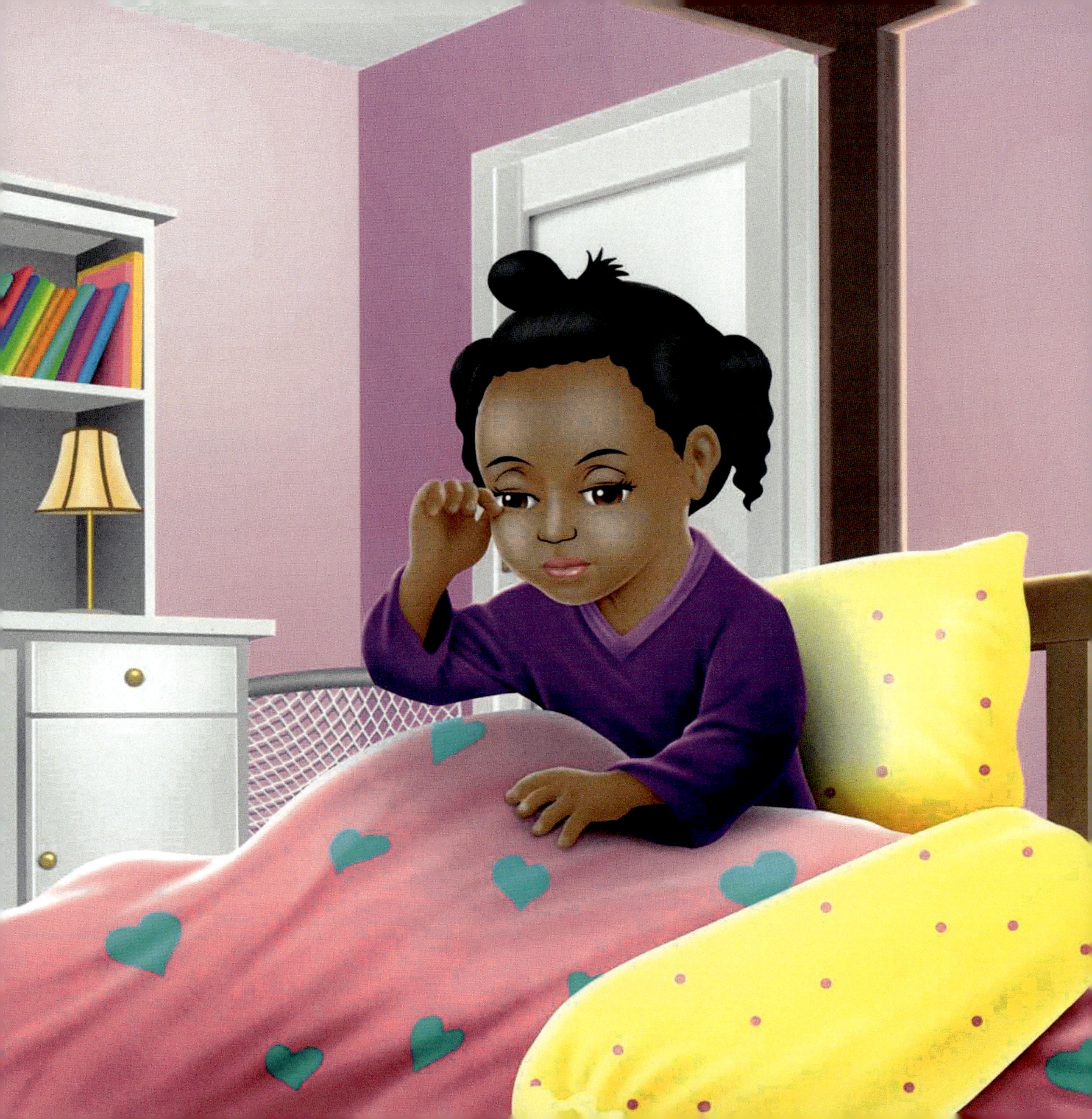

It was a cheerful, bright, Saturday morning and Sherrie was still asleep. Monday through Friday she had to wake up early for school and on Sunday there was church. Saturday was the only day she was allowed to sleep-in a bit late.

Sherrie groggily sat up in her bed, there was a mysterious knock on the door. It was mysterious because she had no idea who it could be. Her 'crew' Jade, Lonny, Cierra, and Latrell, never came over early on Saturdays. They all enjoyed sleeping in and agreed not to come over to the clubhouse before 10:00 am.

Chubbie was running around in circles, barking at the door ready to greet the uninvited guest.   Sherrie rubbed her sleepy eyes and got out of bed to join her mother, Carolyn, and Chubbie at the door to see who had come to visit so early in the morning.

When Carolyn opened the door she saw a frail, little boy leaning on the wall of the house, out of breath and exasperated. He was moving in down the street and needed food and water. He said since they were in the middle of moving, their items had not yet arrived, and he could no longer wait to be refreshed.

"Wait, slow down, what is your name, and where are your parents" asked Sherrie's mom, he spoke quickly and with an accent.

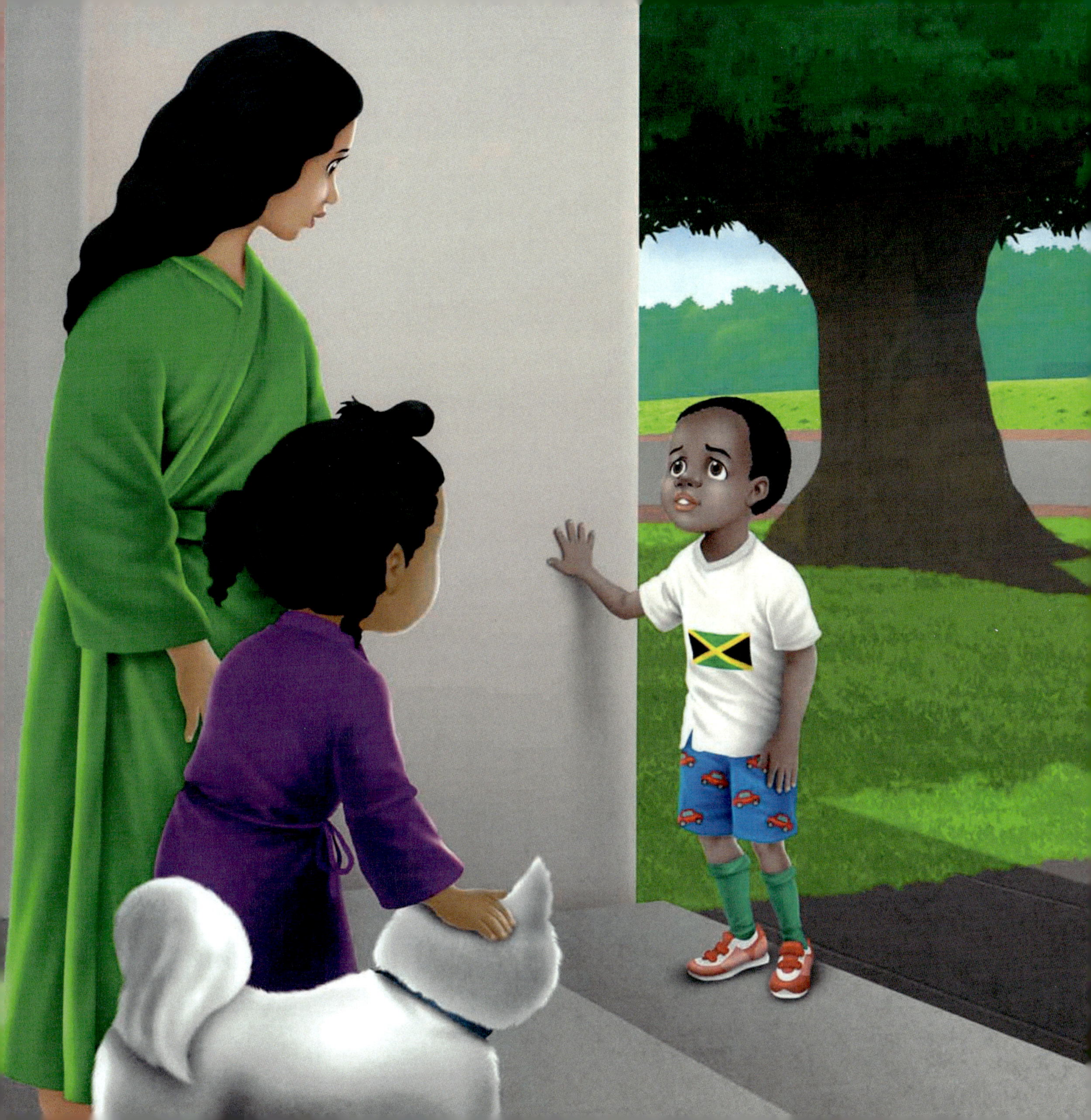

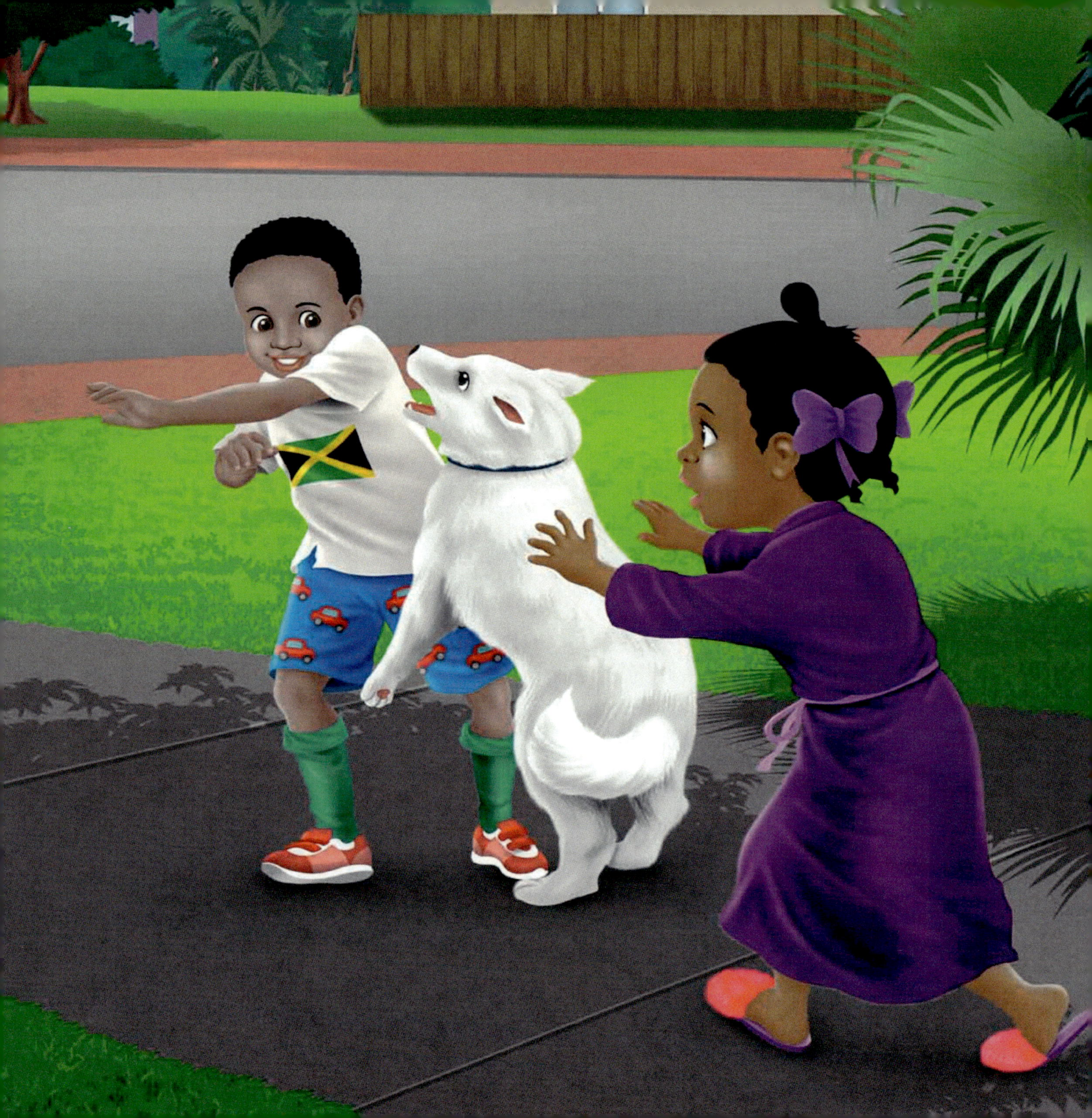

"Oh, I am sorry ma'am my name is Gedion, like the Bible. I just moved here from Jamaica. Immigration was merciless and would not let us bring any food or drink when we arrived, so we are so hungry. My mom said I could come ask for help."

As Gedion told his story, Sherrie noticed he kept taking deep breaths and bending over as if he was hungry and in pain. Chubbie seemed to notice that Gedion was telling "a story," and began jumping on Gedion.

Sherrie quickly pulled him down.

"Chubbie stop that! Gedion is a new guest!"

Gedion laughed. He didn't mind Chubbie jumping on him. He thought Chubbie was introducing himself, but Sherrie knew better, Chubbie was a special dog. Chubbie began barking, non-stop.

"Chubbie, be nice. Gedion is our new neighbor." Sherrie tried to calm Chubbie down, but he was relentless in his attempt to get to Gedion.

"Would you like me to pack some food and drink for your family? We have plenty of leftover chicken and rice from last night's dinner." Sherrie's mother couldn't imagine how famished he and his family must have been. She wanted to help.

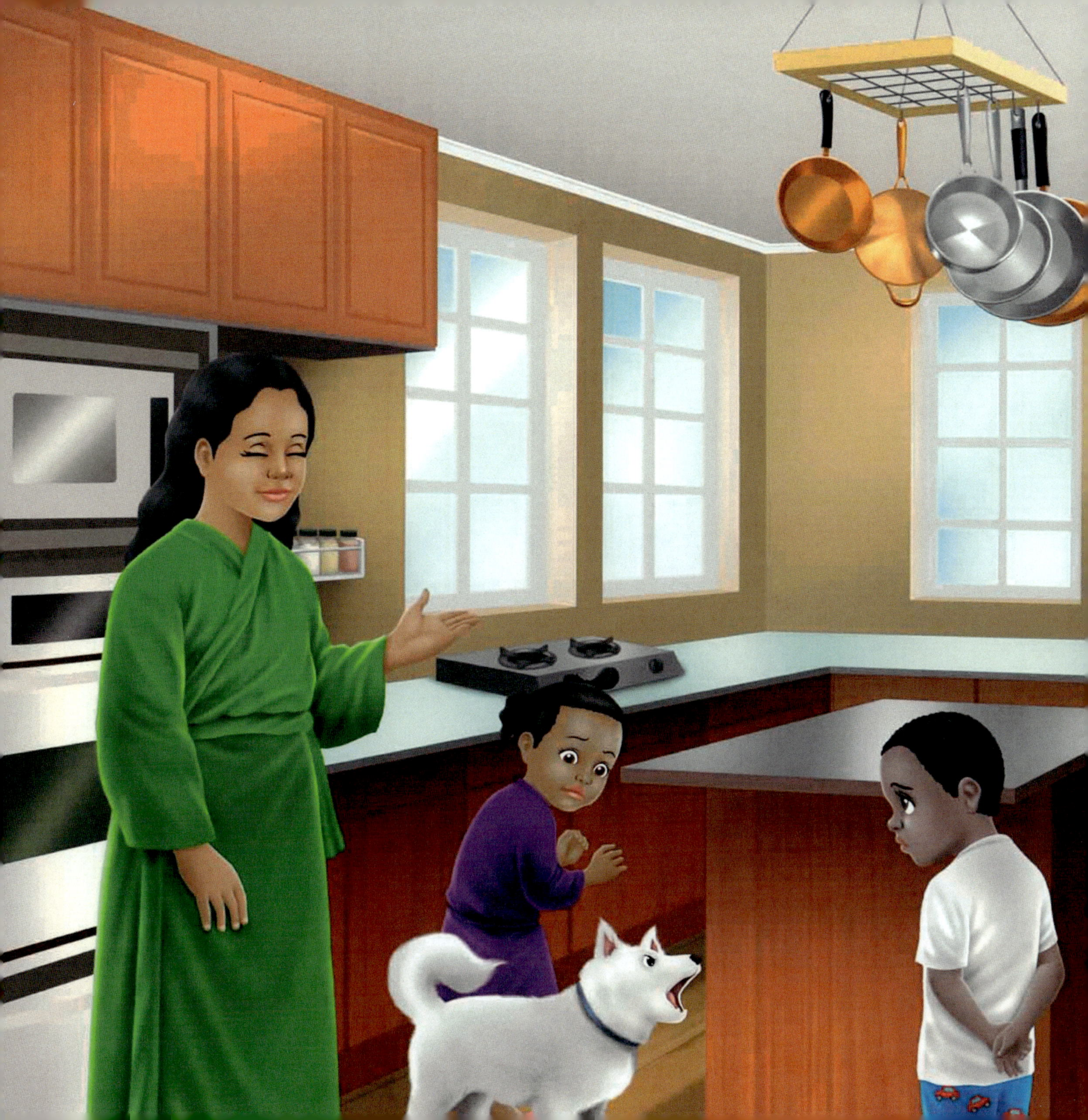

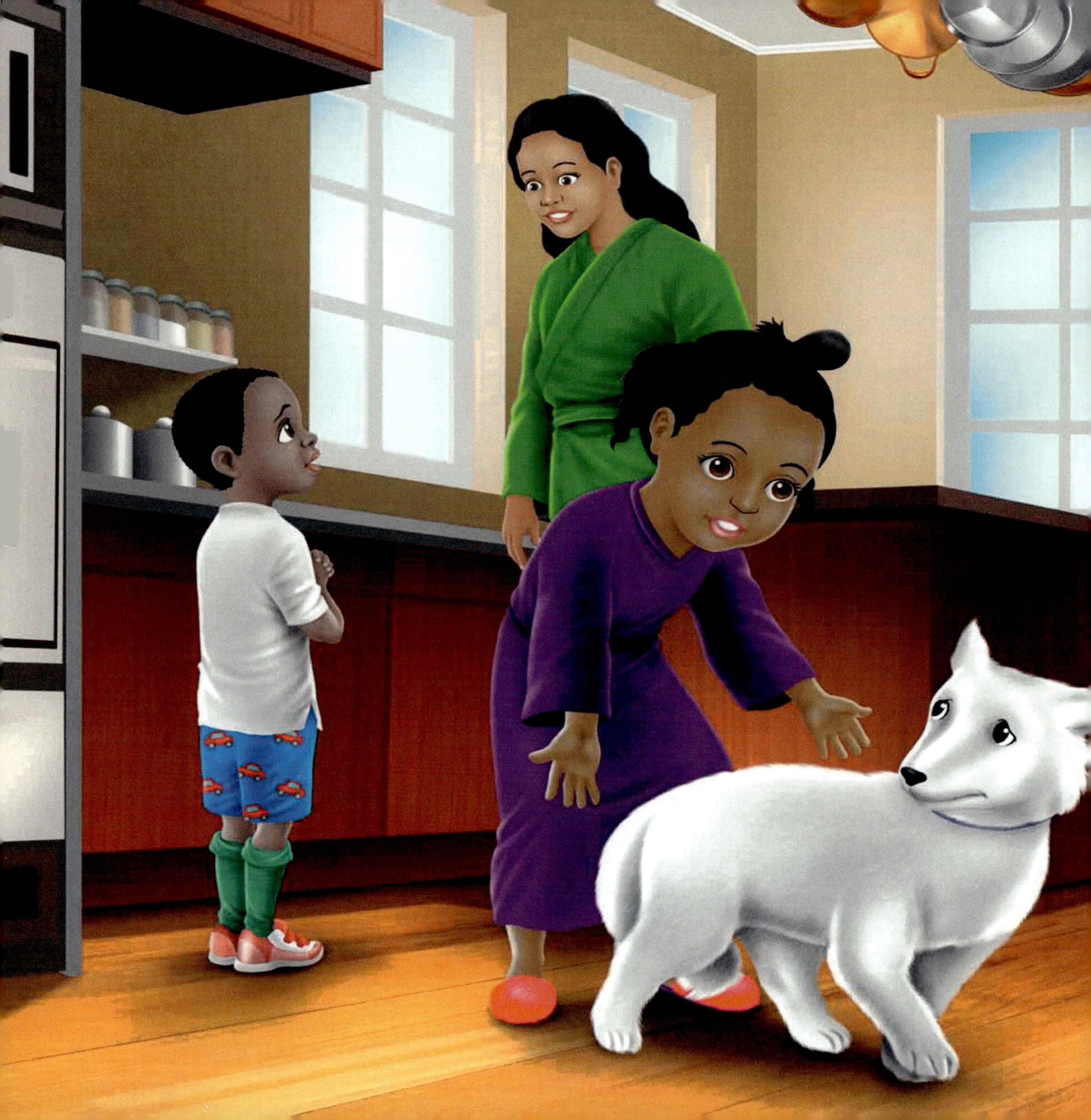

"Oh no, I don't want to be a huge burden… if you could just give me a "lickle" bit of chicken and a soda, that would be fine. I am so hungry from the journey. I have not eaten in two days because we have been moving. We had to hurry and leave our country because we were not safe."

Sherrie laughed to herself at Gedion's pronunciation of the word little.

Chubbie was jumping up and down barking while Gedion told his story. Sherrie had to take Chubbie into her bedroom and close the door to get him to settle down. She had never seen Chubbie get this way before, except with her friend Lonny. Sometimes it took Chubbie awhile to warm up to her friends, but he had never barked incessantly and jumped up on anyone before.

Carolyn prepared and served Gedion a plate of chicken and rice, homemade cornbread, and an ice-cold soda. Gedion sat and ate his food and drank his soda with the biggest smile on his face. Carolyn was pleased to oblige the young boy, but was concerned about the rest of his family, assuming they were just as hungry as Gedion. She absolutely loved to help people in any way she could. Carolyn was a middle school Home Economics teacher, she taught cooking as an art, but to Carolyn, it was also another way to express love through helping others. She enjoyed being a part of the lives of young people; it was her passion.

    Sherrie and her mom sat at the table with Gedion, between bites he continued the sad story of his family's difficult time in Jamaica.

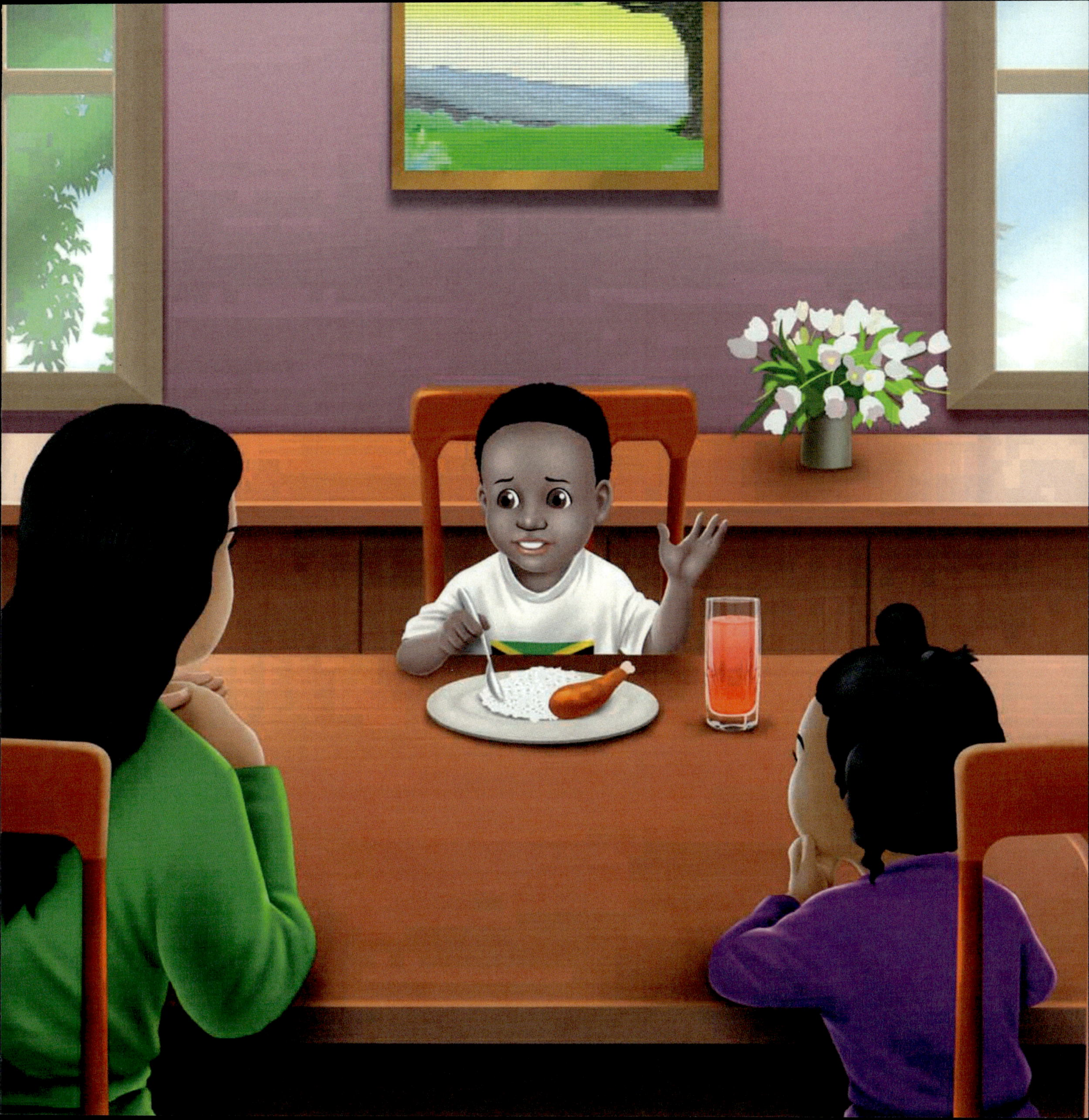

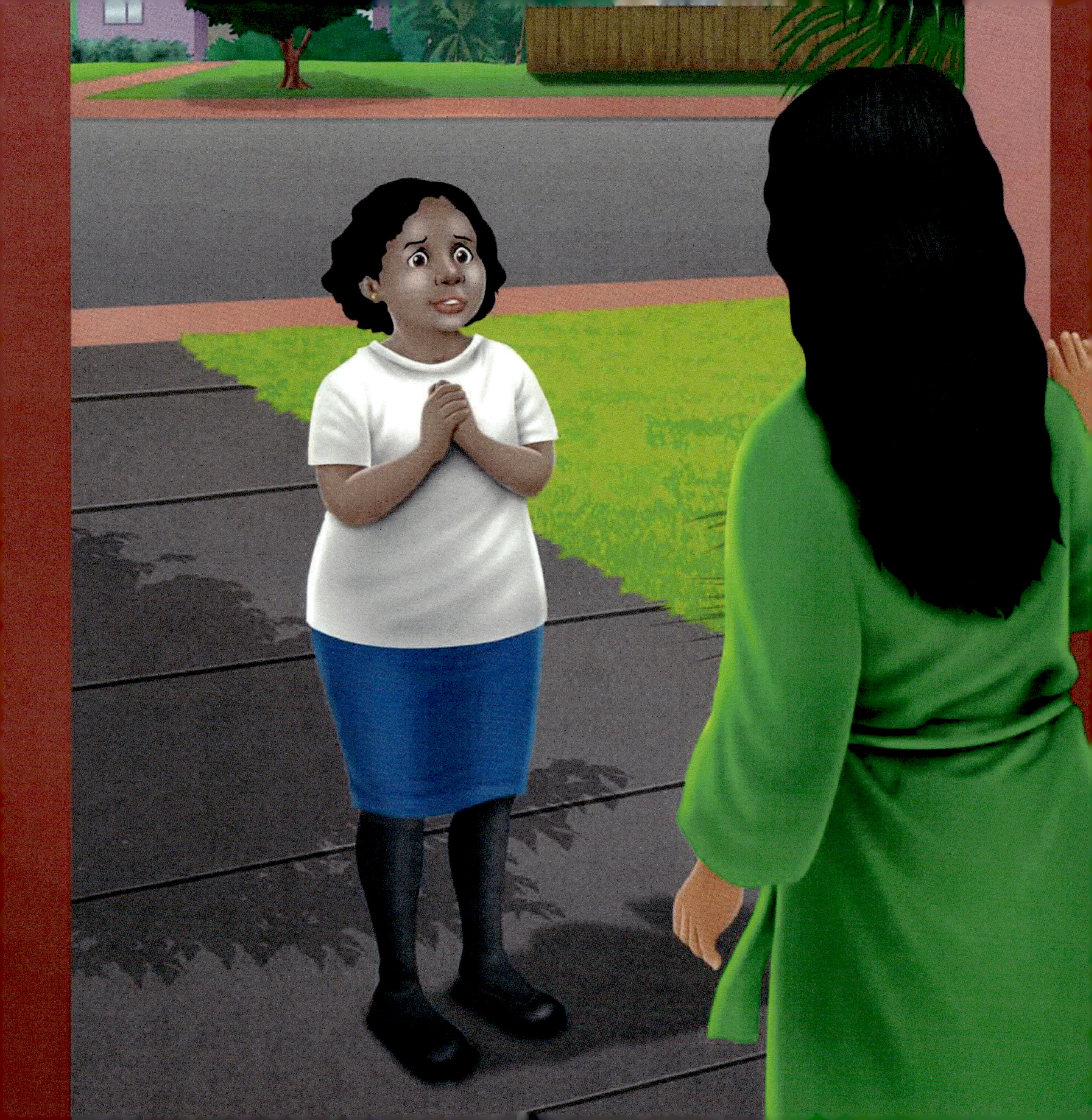

In the middle of his colorful story there were two loud knocks at the door. The next round of desperate knocks, that came before Carolyn could reach the door, were louder. She opened the door to meet the tear-stained face of a frantic mother.

"Good afternoon, I am Sylvia and I just moved in down the street! My son Gedion has gone missing, and I need assistance. Have you seen anyone, or do you think he could have been abducted, who should I call, and what can I do? I am so worried about him. I am so sorry to impose, but you were the first person to answer the door out of all the houses I tried. We just moved here from Jamaica, and we don't know anyone." "Oh Lord, please help me."

Carolyn was saddened by the look of despair in Sylvia's face. She knew how upset she would be if she could not find Sherrie in a new environment. She reached out to console Sylvia, to tell her Gedion was inside, safe, she wanted to ease her mind, but Sylvia was talking a mile a minute.

"Ms. Sylvie, please, I apologize, Gedion showed up about fifteen minutes ago hungry and thirsty pleading for food. I heated up some leftovers and allowed him to sit at the table to get a chance to rest and eat. He showed up out of breath and told us the story of how you had to flee from your country without sustenance for two entire days. My heart broke when I heard your family's story, so I wanted to make sure he had nourishment. Gedion assured me you had sent him for help. I know how hard it is to care for young people and with all of his siblings, in a new country I thought I was being of service. In hindsight, I should have called or come down to meet you before taking him in."

"Gedion," Sylvia bellowed... "com-ya!"

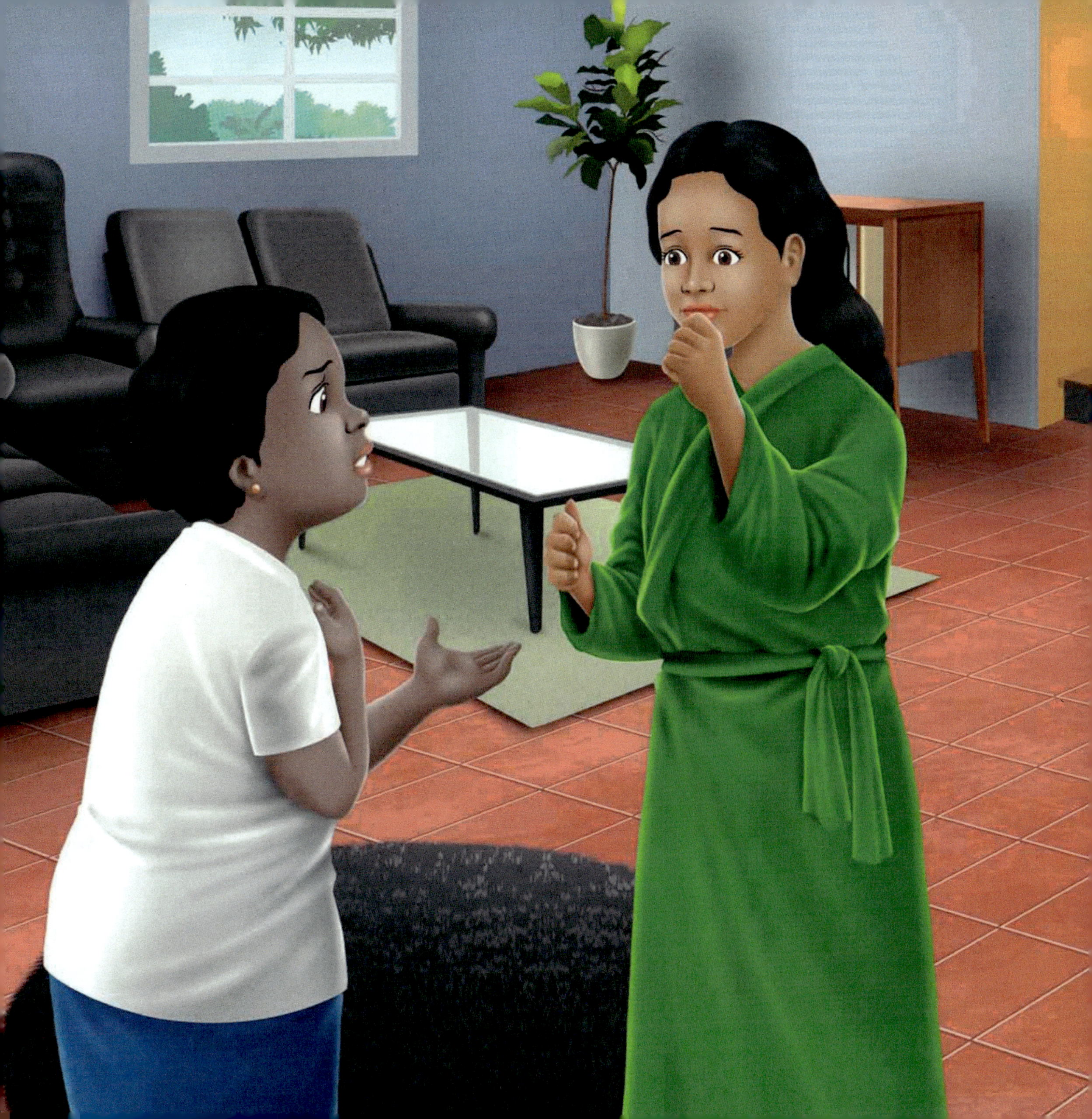

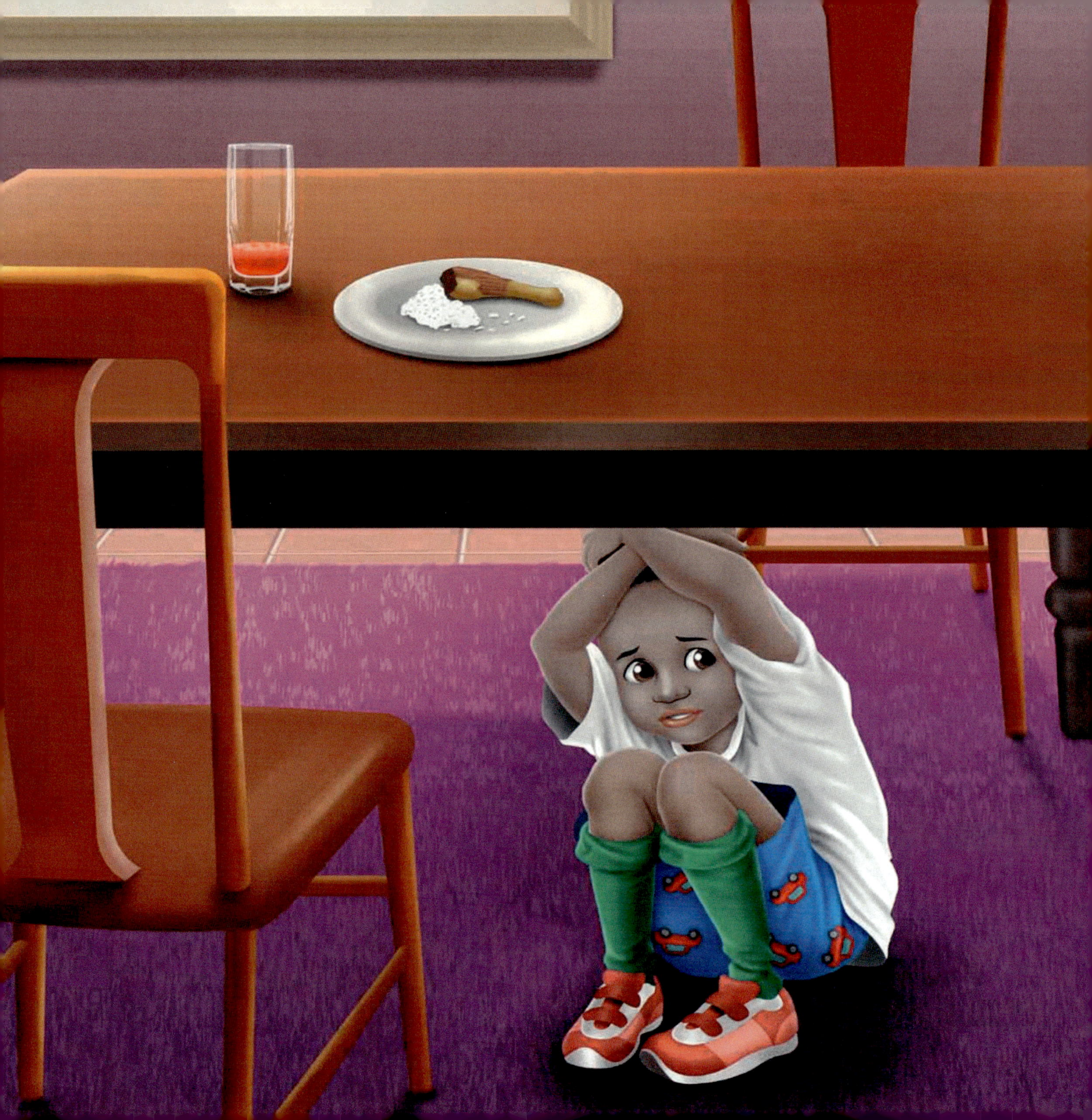

Gedion was frozen stiff. He had gotten under the table to hide when he heard his mother's voice the moment she first entered the house. He had not budged. Sherrie was in the kitchen but was eavesdropping on her mother's conversation with Ms. Sylvia. Sherrie came around the corner and informed them that Gedion had retreated under the table and refused to come out.

Tears streamed down Sylvia's face. They were tears of joy now that she found Gedion and he was safe, but there were also tears that represented the embarrassment she felt in her heart. Gedion often told 'stories' that were not honest.

"What's wrong Ms. Sylvia," asked Carolyn. "Are you still upset that I did not call you? Why won't Gedion come?"

"He is hiding because he has been dishonest." Sylvia replied. "I did not tell him to come ask for help. He was supposed to be unloading items from the car, when he did not come back for some time, I began to worry. He has eaten in the past two days, but since everything is packed up and we have been conserving money through our trip, we have been eating sandwiches. We all could use a hot meal, but Gedion has been constantly complaining. He decided to come down here and fabricate this story to get what he wants to eat. Unfortunately, this is not my first time dealing with his dishonesty. I am having a difficult time with Gedion as he is often not truthful, especially if he believes it will allow him to get his way. I have tried everything to get him to see that his stories could hurt someone one day."

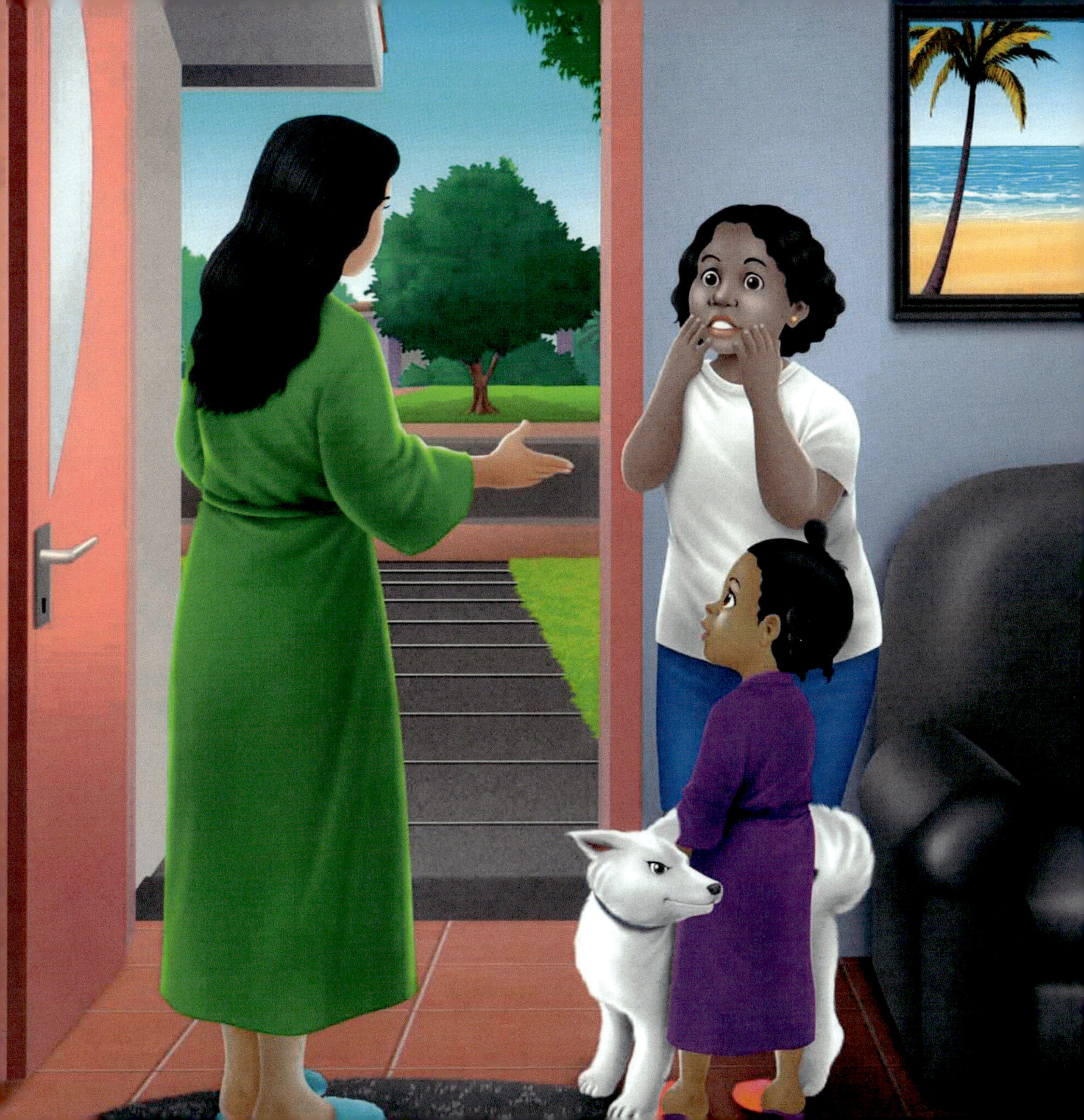

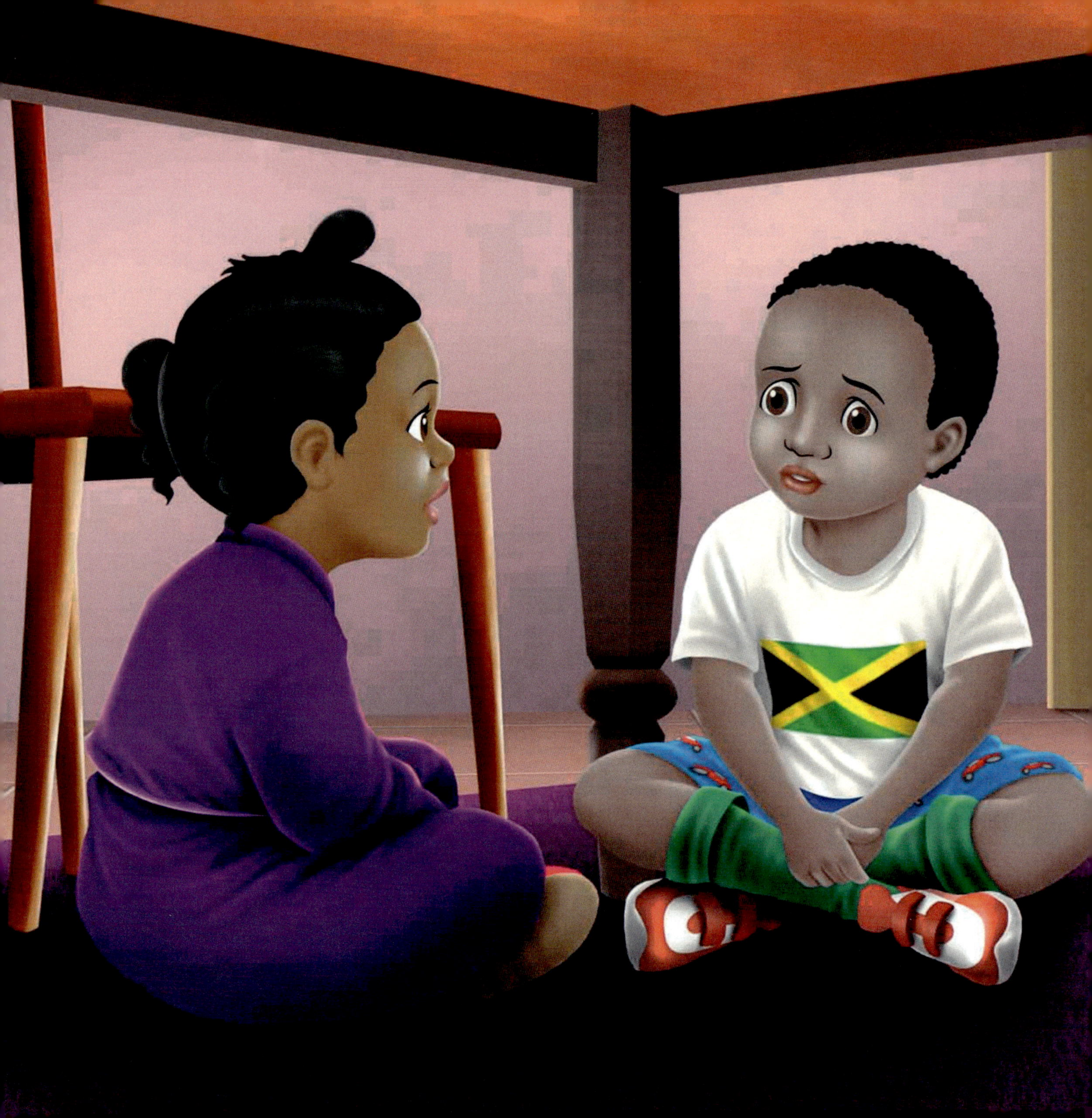

Sherrie had heard enough. *That's why Chubbie was behaving so weird*, she thought to herself as she went to sit under the table with Gedion.

"Why did you tell us so many made-up stories Gedion? Don't you like us?"

He explained to Sherrie that he did not want to live in America. He wanted to go back and live with his dad and cousins in his homeland of Jamaica. Gedion could not take eating any more cold cuts; he longed for some jerk chicken.

"I really was hungry; I just didn't have the patience to wait for my mother to open the boxes so she could cook." Sherrie didn't understand why he would lie, but she convinced him to come from under the table and face his emotional mother.

Sylvia had an angry look on her face when she saw him enter the room.

"Gedion Alexander, we have disturbed Sherrie & her mother enough today, let's go home and finish unpacking."

"Well, we enjoyed your company," said Carolyn, "and you all are welcome anytime. Gedion please bring us more stories, but we prefer the non-fictional type if they are about you and your family." Carolyn gave him a wink when he looked over at her.

Gedion smiled, he could tell there was something different about this family, but he was not sure what the difference was. He felt like he could be honest with them, something told him that Sherrie would be his first new friend, and that made him fill with joy inside. Usually when people found out about his fabricated tales they kept their children away from him afraid they too would pick up the nasty habit of telling lies. He knew they could have been mean to him since he had been dishonest right from the start, but they gave him another chance. This mercy made him feel close to them instantly.

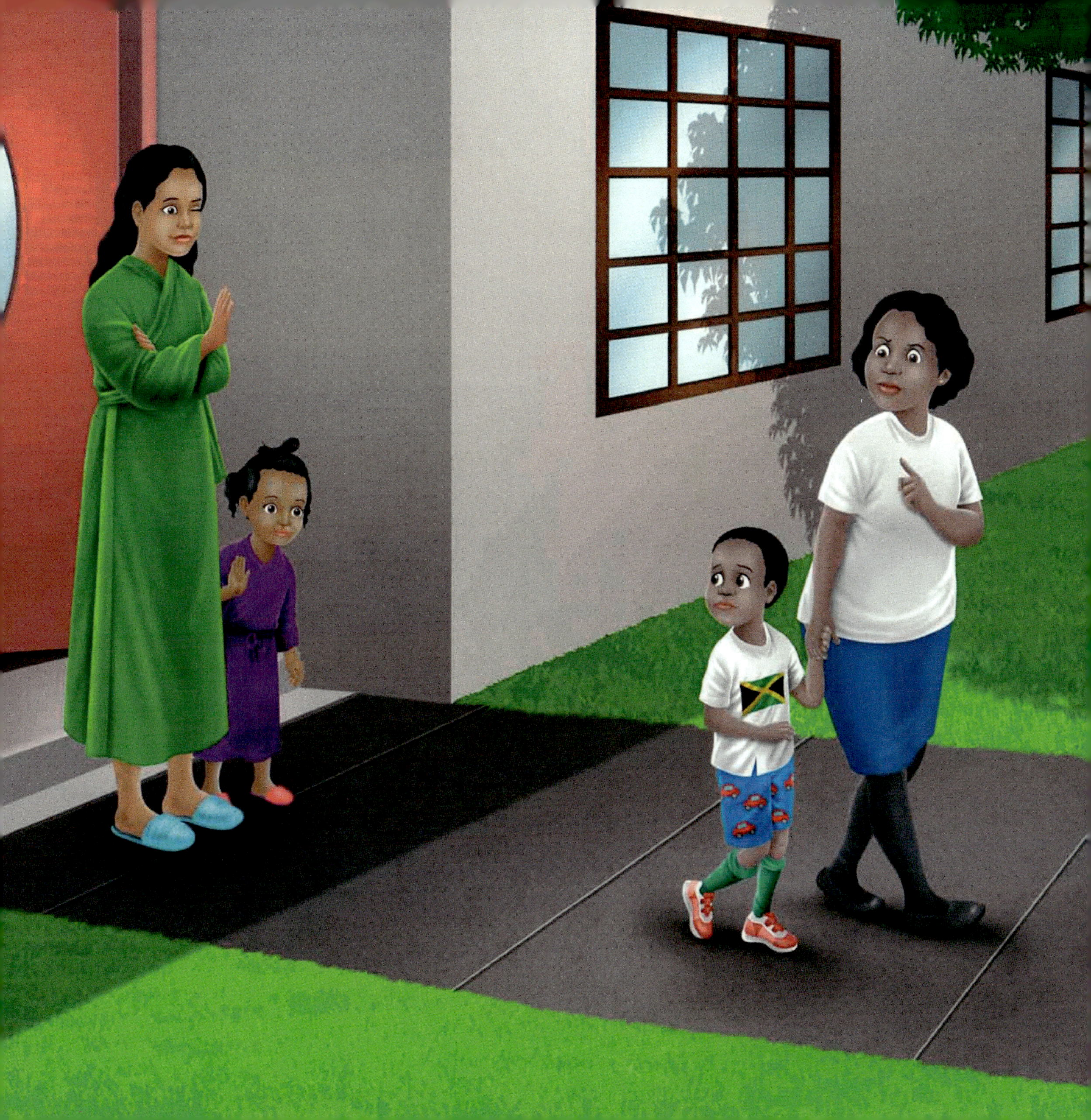

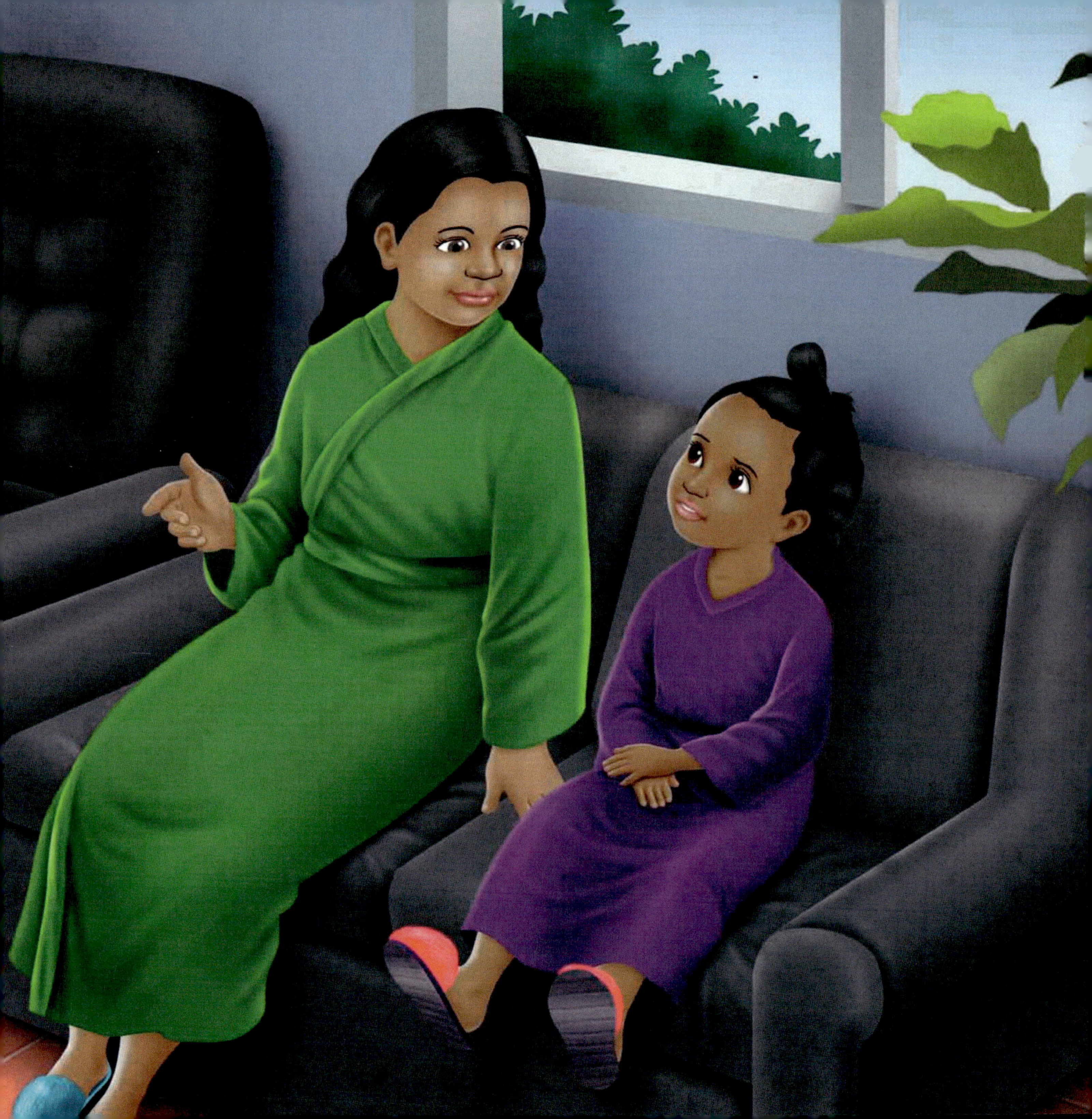

When Gedion and his mother left, Carolyn told Sherrie they needed to talk about what had occurred. She felt there was a lesson to be learned about being honest. Sherrie assured her mother that honesty was very important to her and that she wouldn't make up stories that were not true. They both agreed to forgive Gedion because he deserved another chance and because he was an amazing storyteller.

"Mama I loved hearing about his adventures with his cousins in Jamaica. I am going to tell him what you taught me about using our, powers and talents for good and not evil, so he can help people. Maybe he can write stories." They both laughed.

Sherrie was learning a lot and growing up quickly, her mother was very proud of her.

On Monday Gedion showed up at his new school. Sherrie saw him on the school yard standing alone. Sherrie, followed by her crew, went over to say hello. She introduced Gedion to Jade, Lonny, Cierra, and Latrell. Lonny and Cierra were skeptical, but Jade welcomed him with open arms and Latrell immediately picked up on his accent and began asking him questions about their homeland. Sherrie smiled at the thought of a new crew member and invited Gedion to come over later after school.

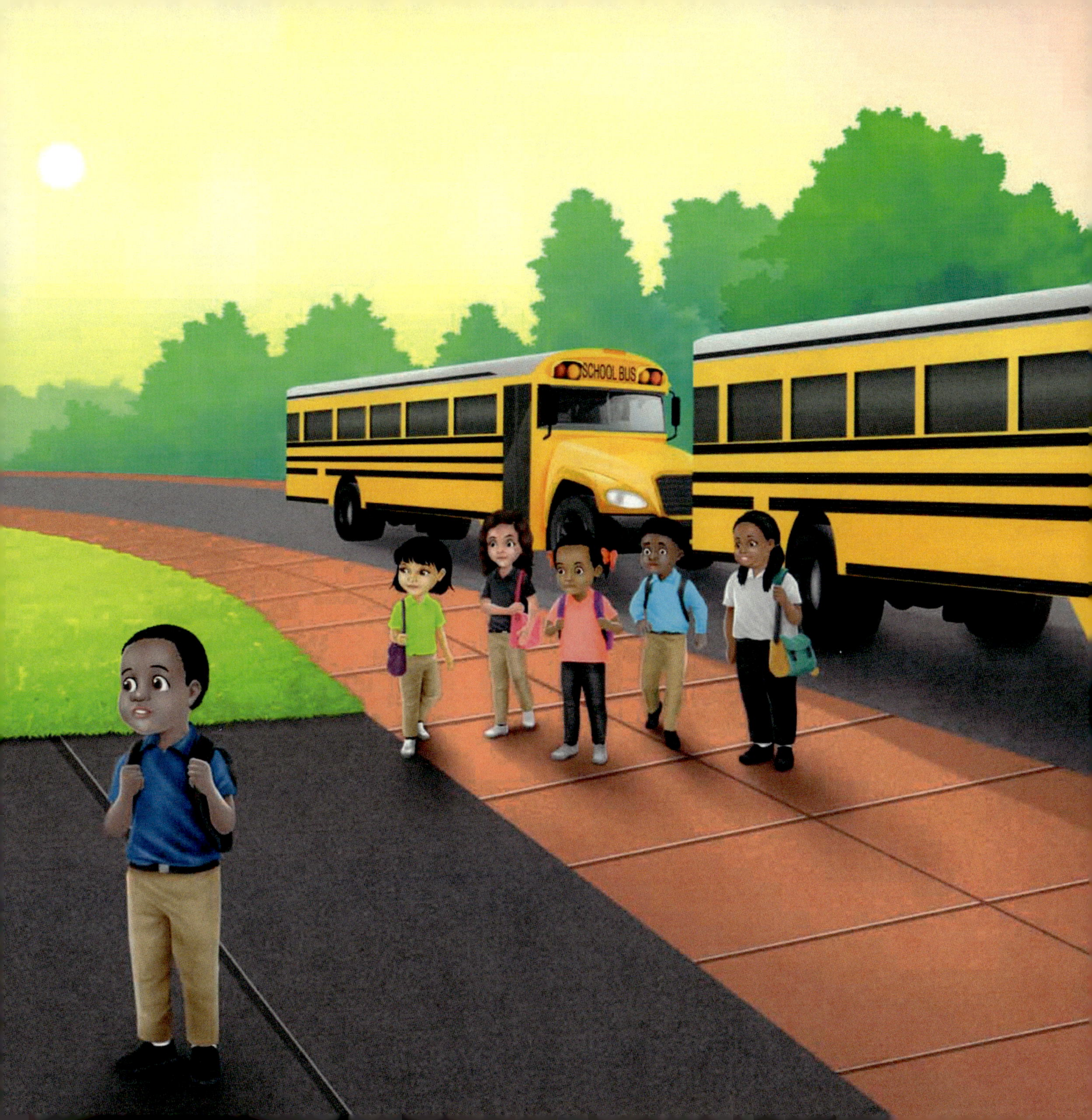
SCHOOL BUS

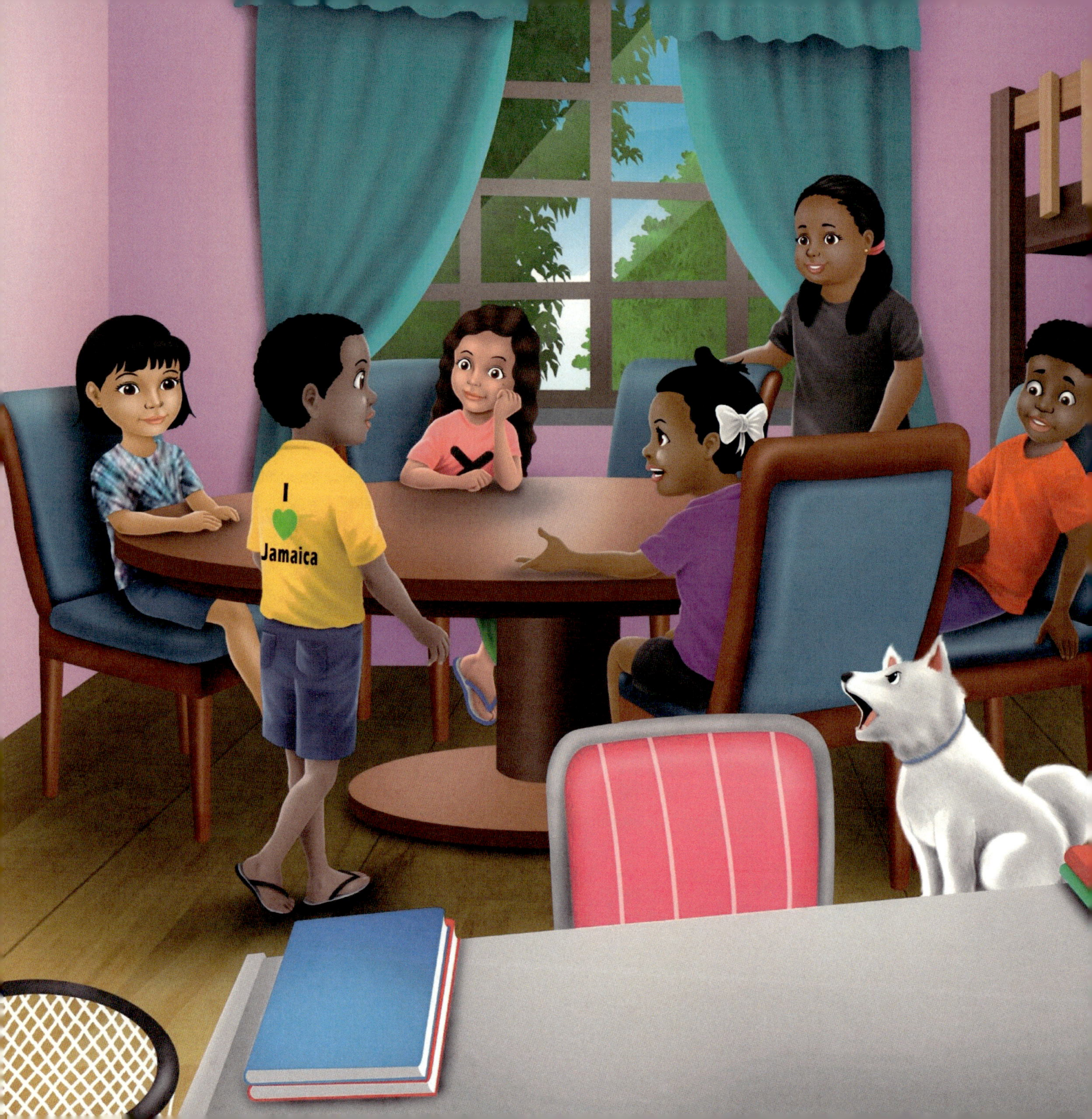
I
Jamaica

After school the crew met up at Sherrie's house, the clubhouse in Sherrie's bedroom. Chubbie barked at Gedion, but not like on Saturday morning.

"I told you he does not like boys. He is racist." Lonny told Sherrie.

"I told you Lonny, that you mean sexist, not racist." The crew laughed because Cierra was always correcting Lonny, and everyone else, but mostly Lonny.

"Chubbie is not either, he loves everyone, he just takes time to warm-up to new people." Sherrie replied.

"Well, why is he following Gedion around barking at him nonstop?" Lonny asked. Sherrie noticed Gedion was telling another one of his fictional stories. As he told untruthful versions of his life, it was as if Chubbie could sense the dishonesty, he barked for the rest or their visit.

That night Sherrie talked to Chubbie asking him why he kept barking at Gedion. As soon as she said the name Gedion, Chubbie barked. Sherrie rubbed Chubbie's head.

"Let's pray Chubbie because we have to accept all of God's children.

Lord, I need Chubbie to like Gedion as You brought both of them in my life as my friends. I know You want us to love each other and be our brother's keeper. Please touch Chubbie and show him how to love Gedion as You love us all." Chubbie barked. "In Jesus Name. Amen."

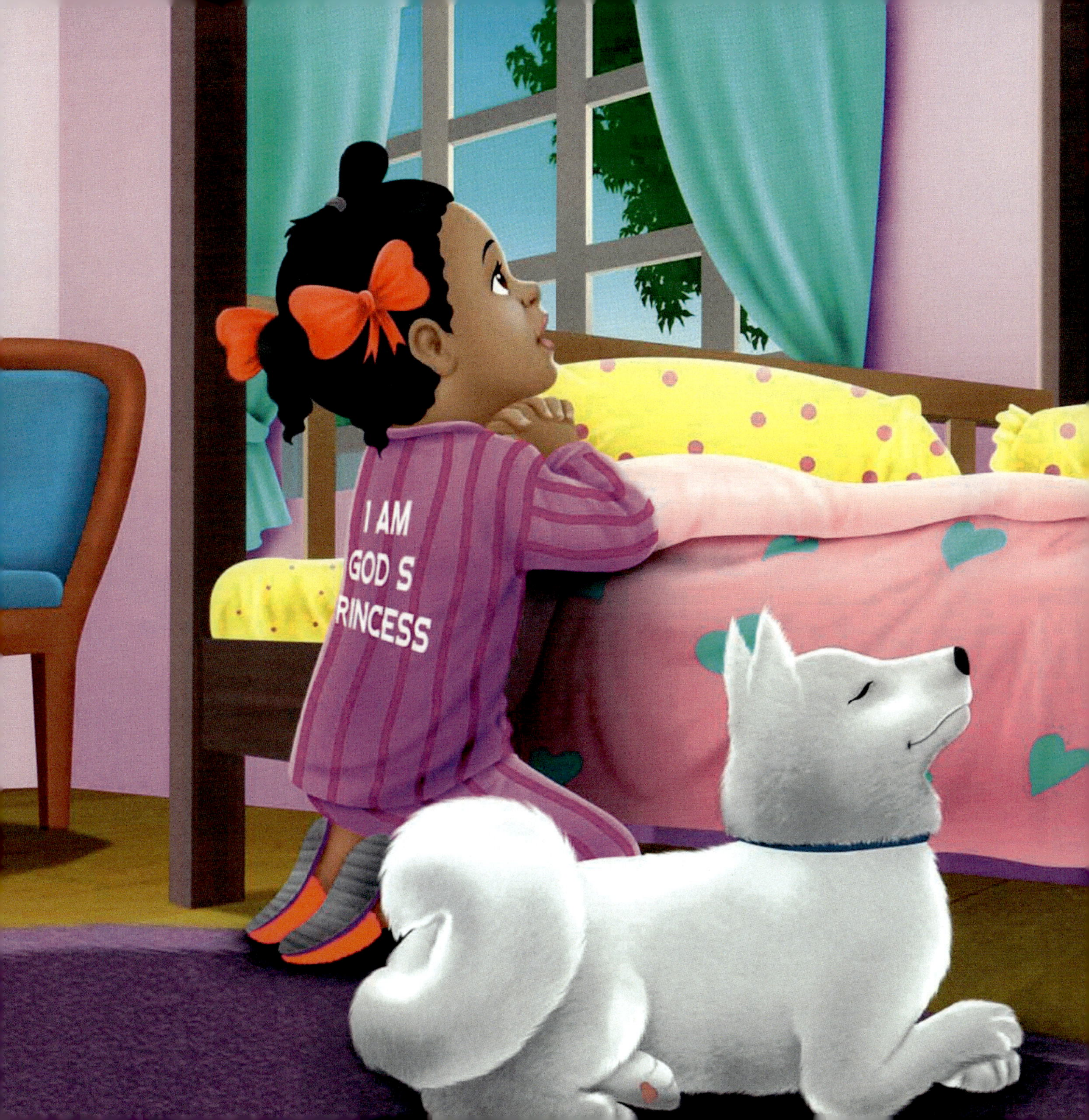
I AM
GOD S
RINCESS

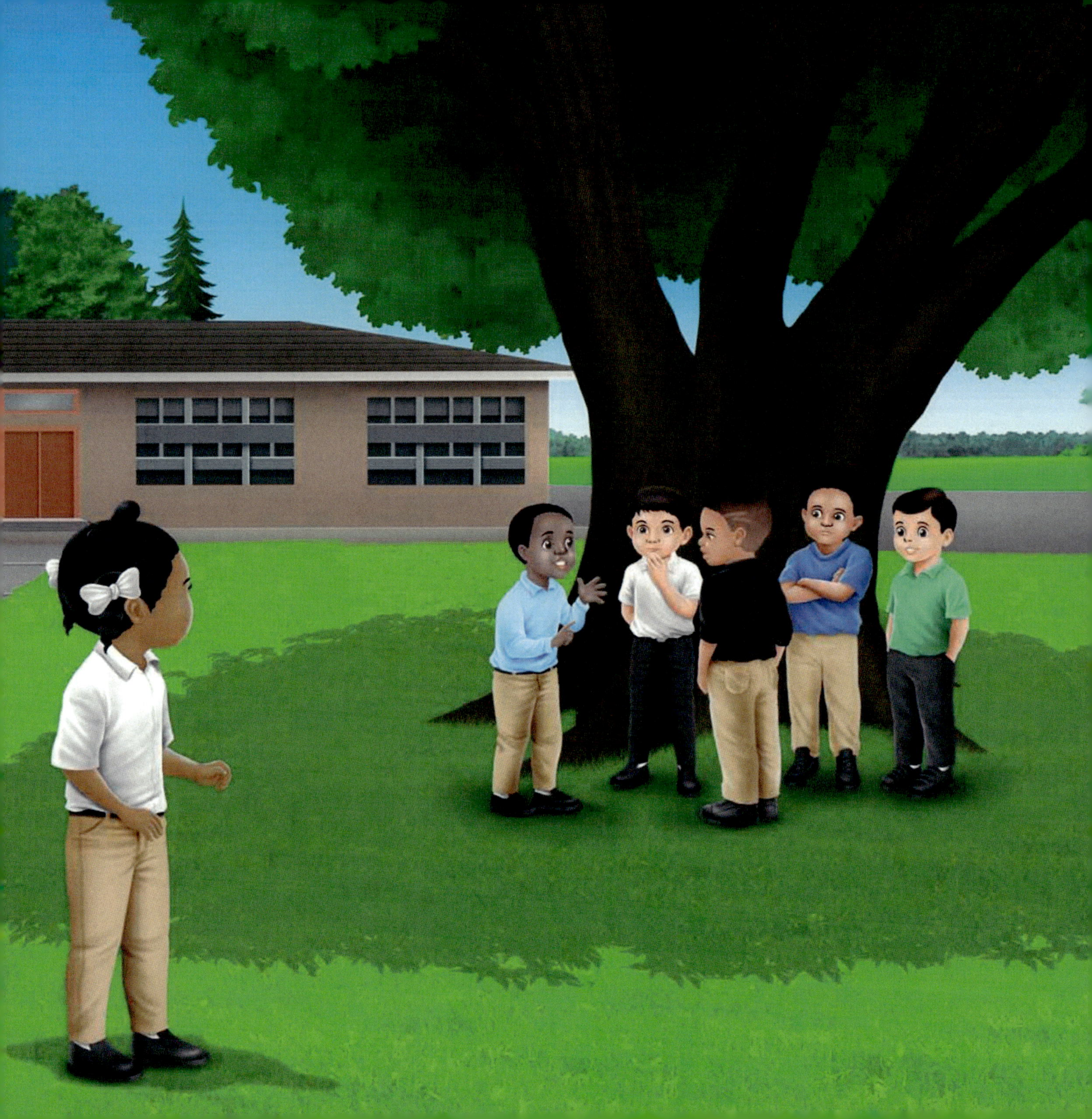

The next school day, Sherrie walked up to Gedion during recess. He was talking to a group of boys. As Sherrie walked up to the group she recognized some of the untruthful stories he had previously told her and her mother. Sherrie was uncomfortable with the deceit and began to walk away. It saddened her that Gedion kept choosing to be untrustworthy. Sherrie knew that she had to do something to help her friend. She prayed last night for God to touch Chubbie, but she forgot to pray for God to change Gedion's heart so he could be honest.

"Why are you leaving Sherrie?" Gedion asked running after Sherrie. "You don't like those boys?" "No that is not it at all Gedion. I am friends with most of the other kids. I didn't want to hear you being dishonest again. You said you would try to be honest. My mother said it is hard to get people to trust you if you are dishonest all the time, especially if you just met them."

"I just want the boys to like me. I am lonely sometimes without my cousins. We played together every day, now I live here, and I have to get these boys to like me so that I will have new friends here to play with me."

"What about my crew? We like you as you are and will play with you if you are a good friend. The clubhouse is open every day and if you tell us the truth we will trust you."

"If you want me to be honest, I will try because I like your crew Sherrie, well, everyone except Lonny. He just stares at me and Chubbie keeps barking at me. They don't like me for me."

"Yes, they do Gedion, Lonny just needs to warm-up to you. He is doubtful of anyone new. Once he has a chance to get to know the real you, you guys will be like brothers. Chubbie is barking at your dishonest stories, not you. If you notice he only barks when you are not truthful. Chubbie was a special gift from God, so he is unique. Unlike other dogs, he can tell when people are not being genuine." They both giggled at how smart and gifted Chubbie was.

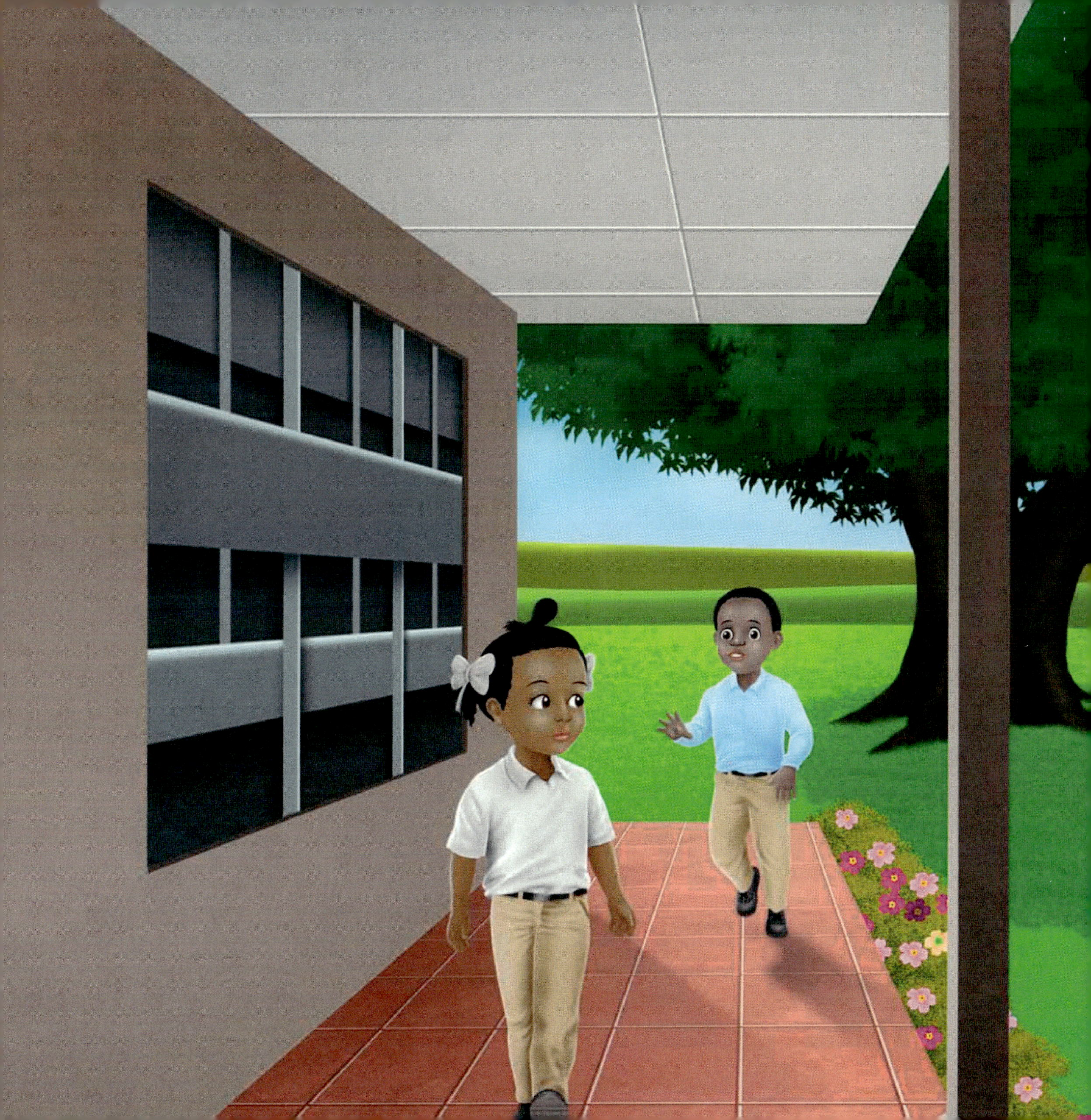

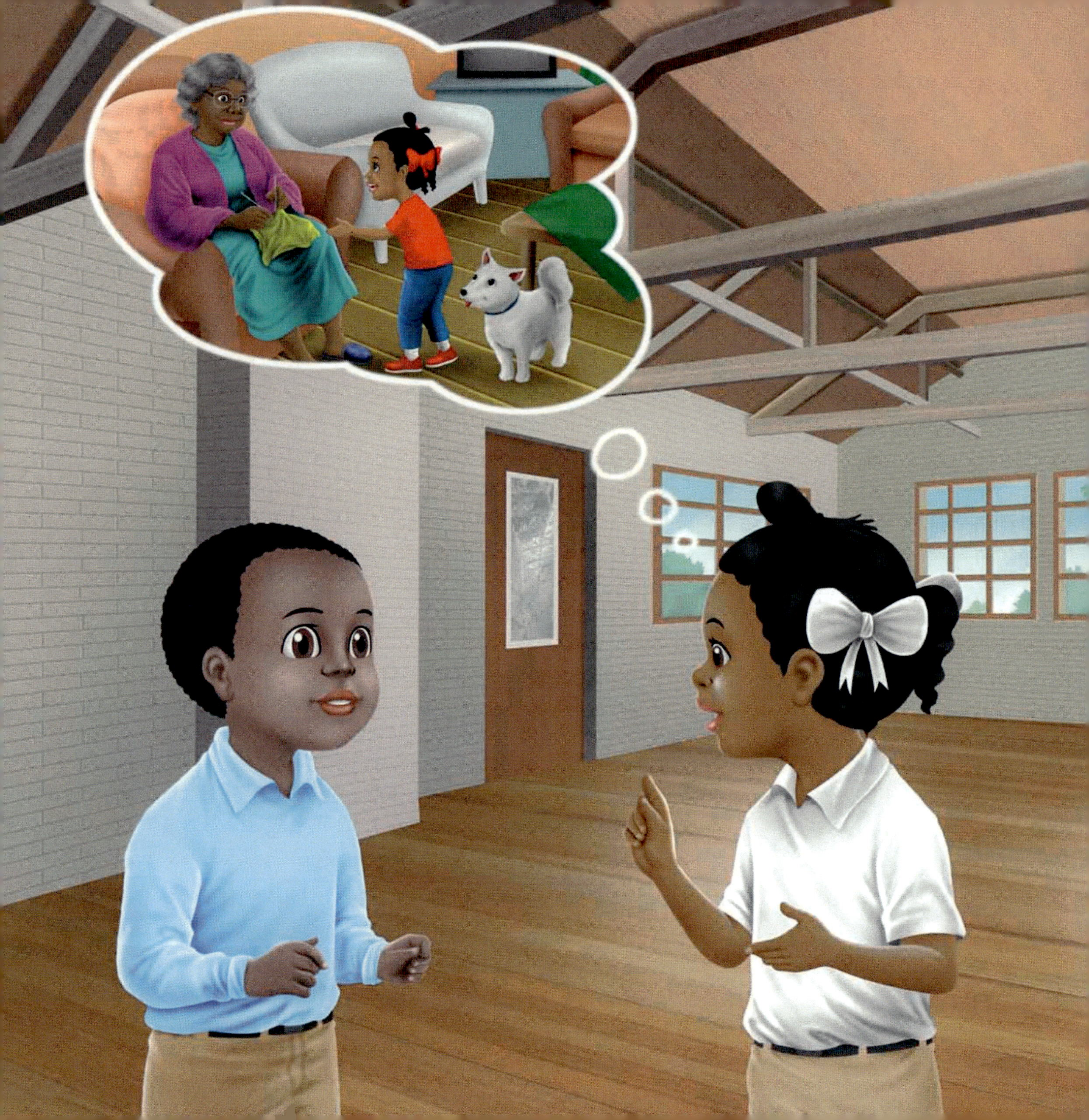

"Are you going to start using your power for good and not evil? You can tell stories for God. You can be a writer one day because your stories are entertaining," giggled Sherrie. Even though she laughed, she really did believe Gedion had a special talent with storytelling!

"I know one day everyone will love you and be your friend if you are honest. My grandma, Alma says honesty is a form of love. When you love someone enough to be sincere, it allows them to love you back. God offered to save a whole city in the Bible if He could find one honest man. The honesty would turn away God's wrath."

"Okay, okay… I will be honest from now on Sherrie, really. It is not going to be easy because I like telling my stories, exaggeration is my middle name, but I have a feeling with you and Chubbie around, I will not have a choice!

THE END….

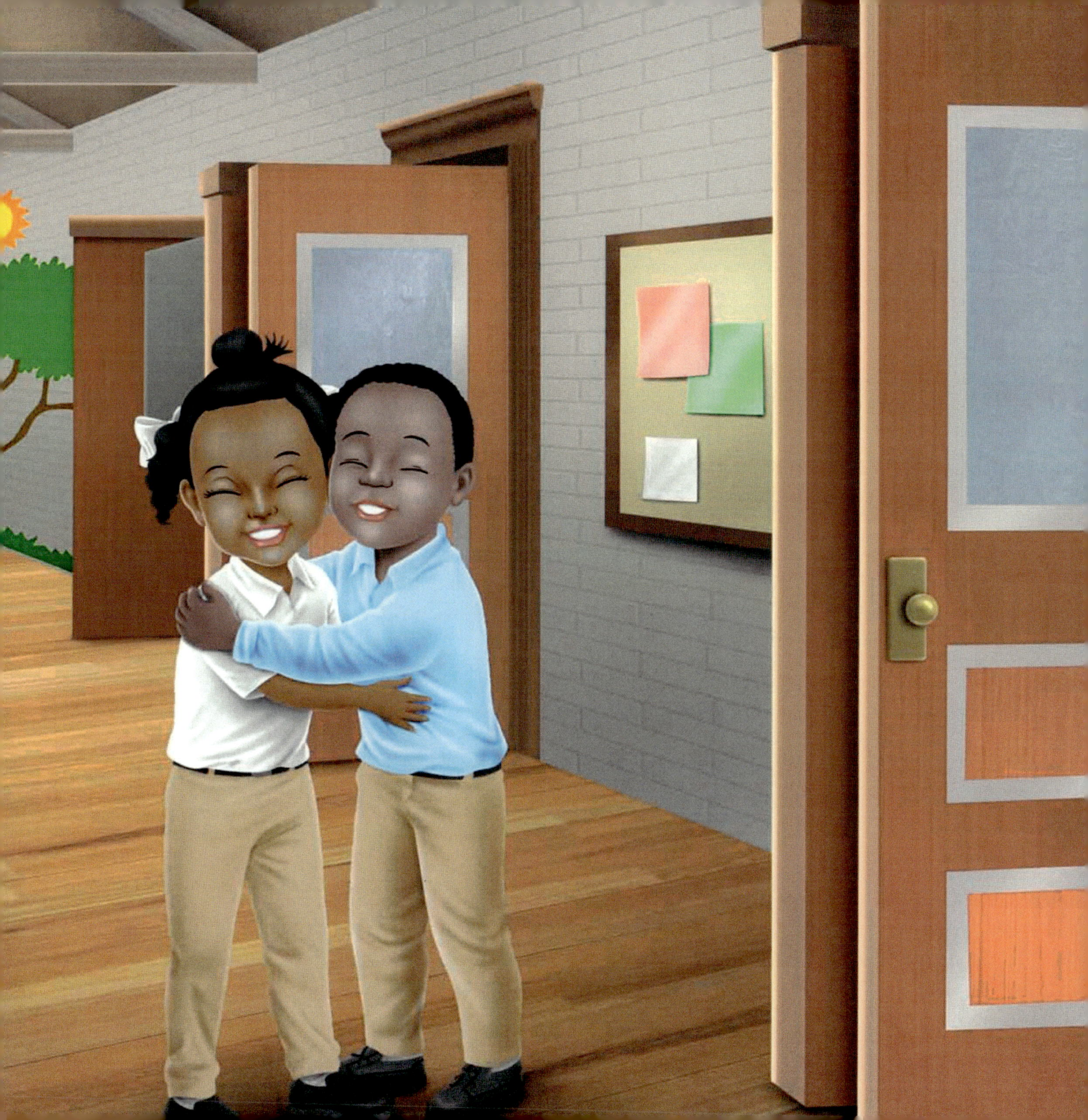

Meet Dr. Sherrie Poitier-Liscombe

In 1994, Sherrie Poitier-Liscombe earned a bachelor's degree in Business Administration, Management from Mercer University in Macon, Georgia. Nine years later in 2003, she earned a Master of Science in School Guidance and Counseling from Nova Southeastern University. During 1997 to 2003 Sherrie Poitier-Liscombe worked as a teacher of middle grades science in Broward County Public Schools.

In 2003, three days after completing the Master of Science program she began the Ph.D. program in Marriage & Family Therapy and was promoted to guidance counselor where she served in that capacity until 2012 when she was again promoted, this time to school counseling director of eight alternative programs, some of which were in jail and juvenile detention centers. Dr. Poitier-Liscombe's life has been dedicated to serving high (at-risk) youth for over 21 years. In these two decades she has forged academic and social/emotional progress in alternative settings while building academic and vocational programming.

In 2017, Dr. Sherrie became a published Children's author, penning a series teaching children good character through the main character's friendships. Sherrie's character is a "peer counselor" who lives her life serving others and through her relationship with friends, family, and God, she embodies character traits that change her environment.

Dr. Poitier-Liscombe has also mentored numerous teachers and staff members through the NESS (New Educator Support System) and now TIER program. During her employment at Broward County Public Schools, Dr. Sherrie Poitier-Liscombe has received numerous awards, accolades, and local recognition. She has implemented various programs and interventions, which have been utilized throughout Broward County. Additionally, Dr. Sherrie was Teacher of the Year 2016-17 and 2017-18 as well as Broward County Public High School Counselor of the Year 2016-17.

Made in United States
Orlando, FL
18 April 2024